Coco Gauff

Major Tennis Champion

by Grace Hansen

Abdo Kids
LEADING BIOGRAPHIES
Kids

Abdo Kids Jumbo is an Imprint of Abdo Kids
abdobooks.com

abdobooks.com

Published by Abdo Kids, a division of ABDO, P.O. Box 398166, Minneapolis, Minnesota 55439.

Printed in the United States of America, North Mankato, Minnesota.

052024

092024

THIS BOOK CONTAINS RECYCLED MATERIALS

Photo Credits: Alamy, Getty Images, Newscom, Shutterstock

Production Contributors: Teddy Borth, Jennie Forsberg, Grace Hansen
Design Contributors: Candice Keimig, Pakou Moua

Library of Congress Control Number: 2023948675

Publisher's Cataloging-in-Publication Data

Names: Hansen, Grace, author.

Title: Coco Gauff: major tennis champion / by Grace Hansen

Other title: major tennis champion

Description: Minneapolis, Minnesota : Abdo Kids, 2025 | Series: Leading biographies | Includes online resources and index.

Identifiers: ISBN 9798384900740 (lib. bdg.) | ISBN 9798384901440 (ebook) | ISBN 9798384901792 (Read-to-me eBook)

Subjects: LCSH: Gauff, Coco, 2004---Juvenile literature. | Women tennis players--Biography--Juvenile literature. | Female athletes--Biography--Juvenile literature. | African American tennis players--Biography--Juvenile literature.

Classification: DDC 796.342092--dc23

Table of Contents

Coco's Beginnings 4

Tennis Talent. 10

More to Come! 20

Career Highlights. 22

Glossary 23

Index 24

Abdo Kids Code. 24

Coco's Beginnings

Cori Dionne "Coco" Gauff was born March 13, 2004, in Delray Beach, Florida. She spent her early years in Georgia with her parents and two younger brothers.

Delray Beach
Florida

Coco's parents were good athletes. They **encouraged** their daughter to play sports. Coco enjoyed soccer, gymnastics, and tennis from a young age.

Coco showed great talent in tennis. When she was 7, her parents left their jobs to support her. The family moved back to Delray Beach in 2011. Coco began training right away.

Tennis Talent

In 2014, Coco won the United States Clay Court National 12-under title. In 2017, she became the youngest US Open girls' finalist in history. She was just 13 years old.

US OPEN
2017
FINALIST

In March 2019, Coco made her **WTA debut** at the Miami Open. She recorded her first professional **match** win.

Barilla

In her Wimbledon **debut**, Coco defeated Venus Williams. She made it through to the fourth round. At 15, Coco became the youngest player to do this since 1991.

In 2022, Coco finished runner-up at the French Open. In August of that year, Coco ranked number 1 in doubles in the **WTA** rankings.

BNP PA

Finally, at the 2023 US Open, Coco sealed her first **Grand Slam** title! She won seven **matches** in all.

More to Come!

Coco accomplished a lot before the age of 20. The world is excited to see what she will do in the years to come.

Career Highlights

March 2019 — Gauff makes her **WTA debut** at the Miami Open and wins her first WTA **match**.

July 2019 — Gauff receives a wild card slot play at Wimbledon. She beats her idol Venus Williams in the first round.

October 2019 — Gauff wins her first WTA Tour singles title at Australia's Linz Open at 15 years and seven months of age.

2021 — Gauff makes the USA Olympic Tennis team but cannot play due to illness.

2022 — Gauff reaches her first major singles final at the French Open.

August 2023 — Coco wins her first WTA 1000 title at the Cincinnati Open.

September 2023 — At age 19, Coco wins her first **Grand Slam** title. She is the youngest woman to win the US Open since Serena Williams.

September 2023 — Gauff reaches the rank of number 3 in the world in singles by the WTA.

Glossary

debut – to present to the public for the first time.

encourage – to give help, support, or approval.

Grand Slam – winning all four major championships in tennis in a calendar year. The four major tournaments are the Australian Open, the French Open, Wimbledon, and the US Open.

match – the overall contest, usually decided by the best two-out-of-three sets.

WTA – short for the Women's Tennis Association.

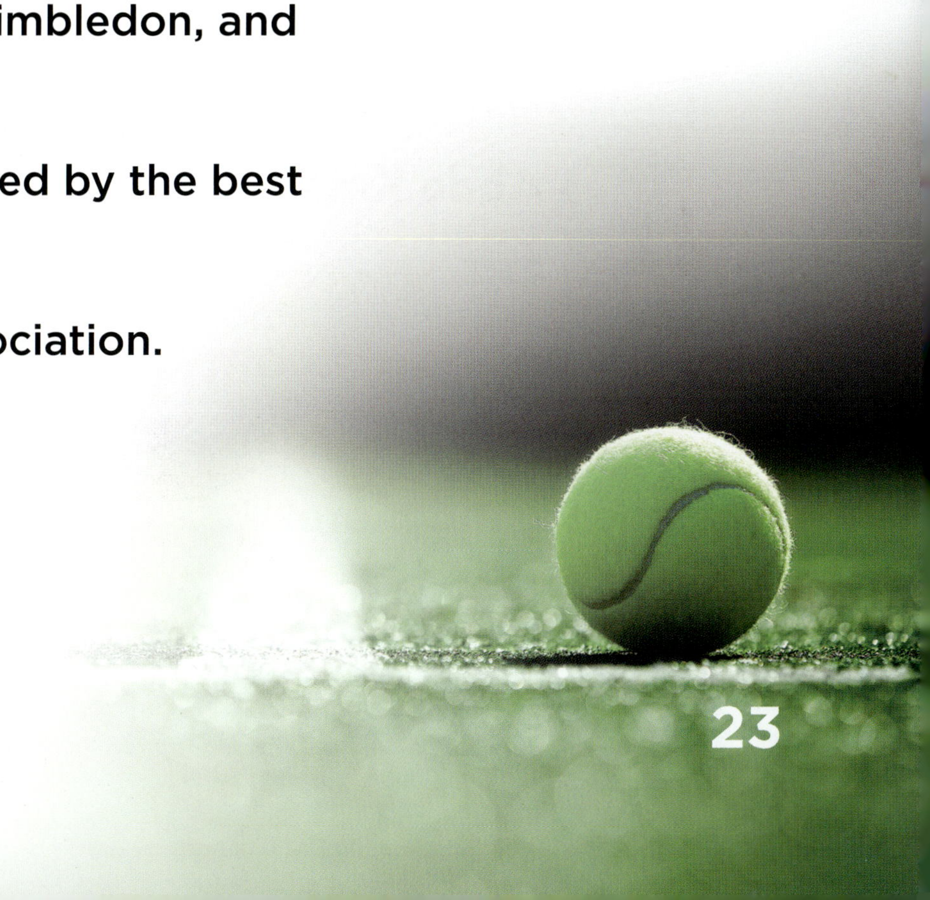

Index

birth 4

childhood 4, 6

Delray Beach, Florida 4, 8

family 4, 6, 8

French Open 16

Grand Slam 18

Miami Open 12

tournaments 10, 12, 14, 16, 18

US Open 10, 18

Williams, Venus 14

Wimbledon 14